Woman Words

A Journal for My Self

HAZELDEN®

First published April, 1990

ISBN: 0-89486-713-X

Printed in the United States of America.

Designer: Maria Mazzara
Illustrator: Marilynn Anderson

Editor's Note:

Hazelden Educational Materials offers a variety of
information on chemical dependency and related areas.
Our publications do not necessarily represent
Hazelden or its programs, nor do they officially speak
for any Twelve Step organization.

The quotations contained on each of the pages have
been compiled from written contributions of women
authors who have been published by Hazelden.
Hazelden reserves the right to publish these quotations
in blank journal format.

Thank you, women authors of Hazelden,
for your joyous and complete participation
in the process of making this journal a reality.

Practiced consistently, new habits become who I am.

Lin Andrukat

*Healing requires getting rid of old baggage. I want to achieve
the gift of a blank page, with a pencil poised in my own hand
to redraw my life as it unfolds each day.*

Jeanne Engelmann, <u>Women and Spirituality</u>

*Our own patient and steady desire to grow, fed by the love and
kindness of others, will not be stopped by anything or anyone.
Our own gentleness is a powerful force in our lives. It is like the
gentle flower that grows through granite.*

Patricia Hoolihan

The older I get, the less I must live up to society's definition of "women"...and the more woman I become.

Martha Cleveland

Nobody can get my goat if I don't show them where it's tied.

Stephanie Abbott

One step at a time may seem too slow some days, but it gives me a chance to see where I'm going and increases my chance of getting there in one piece.

Kay Marie Porterfield, <u>Keeping Promises</u>

Every relationship is a teacher. If I don't learn the lesson, the teacher will come back.

Brenda M. Schaeffer

*Forgiveness is, ultimately, the way I show greatest love for myself.
It frees me from the burdens of hate, anger and resentment.*

Mary Y. Nilsen

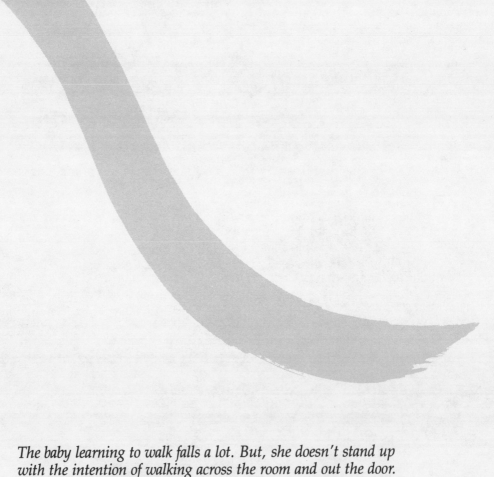

The baby learning to walk falls a lot. But, she doesn't stand up with the intention of walking across the room and out the door. She learns in little bits and pieces. As skill and confidence grow, she practices over and over again, going a little farther each time, gaining power over her own legs, . . . and over her own little world.

Kathleen Rowe

I will give myself the gift of forgiveness.

Harriet Hodgson

When time alone is not what I want, it may be what I need.

Carol Slade

The moment I realized that God has no gender marked a spiritual breakthrough for me. Still, I deal with a sense of shame that comes from being female in a culture that says God is male.

Jane Nakken

*Grace is when we notice the near-misses we survived
instead of the wishes that didn't come true.*

Nancy Hull-Mast

We can't find solitude until we face our emptiness.

Marilyn J. Mason

Assuming financial responsibility for myself is an attitude.
Taking care of money is part of life.

Melody Beattie

There is a purpose for our existence which, at times, transcends human understanding. For some of us, the purpose is readily apparent. For others of us, however, the meaning of our existence and of certain events may become clear only at some future time.

Aphrodite Matsakis, <u>Compulsive Eaters and Relationships</u>

Listen to the melody of your body—the sighs, hisses, groans, cricks, cracking of knuckles, sniffles, clapping, slapping, rubbing, walking, licking, laughing. Sing along.

Pat Samples

"I'm only human" is no longer my excuse...it is my goal.

Joan Malerba-Foran

Today I will experiment. I will pretend to be a spiritual being living a human life.

Martha Cleveland

I keep my valuables in a 'safe deposit box'—my heart. My
valuables are: my feelings, my sense of self, my trust in people,
my vulnerabilities, my ability to risk exposure, my desire to grow
and change, my pride, my dignity.

Amy Dean

Learning to love invites my full attention. I do not need to do it perfectly, but today I can deepen my commitment to those I love.

Anonymous, <u>Inner Harvest</u>

*Perhaps hope is simply an openness to good things
beyond our imagining.*

Carol Slade

Oh, Sorrow,
when we finally name you
we finally let you

let us go

Roseann Lloyd,
"Oh," <u>Tap Dancing for Big Mom</u>

Intimacy means that I will tell you when
your behavior hurts me deeply.

Nancy T.

So often I have listened to everyone else's truth and
tried to make it mine. Now, I am listening deep inside
for my own voice and I am softly, yet firmly,
speaking my truth.

Liane Cordes

If there is a solution to the problem, why worry?
If there's no solution, why worry? Worry is wasted
emotional energy and time.

Carolyn White

Our experiences with others aren't by chance.
Fellow travelers are carefully selected by our inner self.

Anonymous, <u>Each Day a New Beginning</u>

Once conflict has arisen, we are kidding ourselves if we think it can be ignored. We can confront it now, or we can wait for it to come back and haunt us later.

Linda Riebel

Women are taught to internalize problems—to look inside themselves and see what's "wrong" with us. I think we need to give more attention to the external—fighting the systems that oppress us.

Dana L. Wilde

*In a storm, it is the tree that bends with the wind
that survives to grow tall.*

Brenda M. Schaeffer, <u>Is It Love or Is It Addiction?</u>

I can have my way more often if I have more than one way.

Stephanie Abbott

Over time, the choices we make to grow enhance our self-confidence and sense of control so that we feel safer than before. It's one of life's paradoxes that to feel secure, we need to risk ourselves against the unfamiliar.

Patricia Roth Wuertzer

Grief is an ocean that pulls me under, tumbles me, scrapes me up and spits me out on a new beach, three inches taller.

Stephanie Ericsson

*My goal is to become a channel of love and power
to others simply by living who I am.*

Mary Y. Nilsen

When someone tells me to "face reality", I remember that beauty is just as real as ugliness, love is as real as hate, and happiness is just as real as sorrow.

Kathleen Rowe

*When I haven't given up my needs in order to get things done,
I have taken care of myself.*

Patricia Roth Wuertzer

My sense of balance depends on my sense of humor.

Joan Malerba-Foran

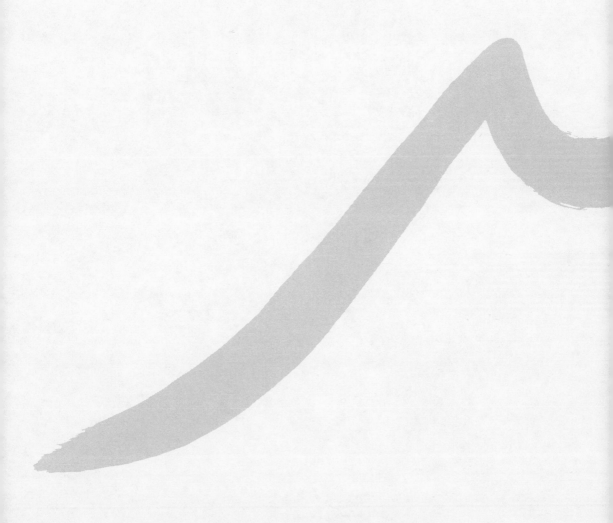

Healing can occur when I see my family of origin as just a vessel to bring me into new spiritual growth, rather than as the predictor of all my life's work.

Dr. Judi Hollis

When I'm out in nature, I feel whole, peaceful, at one with
everything around me. I can feel the moccasined feet of Indians
from earlier centuries quietly trodding the earth beneath my feet.
I see the brittle shell of the crab on the shore and know it fed some
other sea animal in a natural life-and-death chain of events.
And I know I'm a link in that same chain.

Jeanne Engelmann, <u>Women and Spirituality</u>

*Faith is not an option for me. It is a must
for any kind of lasting, loving self-esteem.*

Liane Cordes

Fear is a warning that a rule is about to break.

Linda Riebel

*I'm not sure I'm ready to move outward yet. I'm still sinking
in my roots, loosening and fertilizing the soil, re-potting myself.
Eventually I'll stretch my branches again, but for now
I'll just take some time to regenerate.*

Pat Samples

*If I don't know someone well enough to tell them I don't feel
like being sexual, I probably don't know them well enough
to be sexual with them in the first place.*

Kristin Kunzman

Our deepest beliefs, attitudes, and expectations find their way into the realities of our lives.

Veronica Ray

Give anger its place—and place anger where it belongs.

Sefra Kobrin Pitzele

Oh, Wicked Mother of the Kingdom of Silence,
I have obeyed you
long enough.

Roseann Lloyd,
"Exorcism of Nice," <u>Tap Dancing for Big Mom</u>

*Mourning is the constant reawakening
that things are now different.*

Stephanie Ericsson

Food is not love.

Anonymous, <u>Food for Thought</u>

*It is helpful for me to remember that life's problems are usually
transitory. If I find this hard to believe, I can ask myself:
Ten years from now what difference will (this problem) make?
Just how important is this to my peace of mind and serenity?*

Lin Andrukat

*I stand in that uneasy place of waiting.
It is a necessary uncertainty
and makes room for the new.*

Pat Samples

When must I detach? When it seems the least likely or possible thing to do.

Melody Beattie

Awareness and a deep honesty are the roots of a recovering,
spiritual life. Such a life embraces a larger vision. It allows us
to look at our darker, more hidden truths, the underside of leaves.

Patricia Hoolihan

*Here-and-now living allows acceptance of the past
without guilt and less preoccupation with the future.*

Dr. Barbara McFarland and Tyeis L. Baker-Baumann,
<u>Sexuality and Compulsive Eating</u>

My real purpose is to love. That's all.

Jane Nakken

In learning to trust myself, I need to remember "I know more than I think I know".

Nancy T.

*If I can support myself with love through the small crises
of everyday life, I will strengthen myself for the big crises
which are a part of every human life.*

Jane Rachel Kaplan

In order to learn, risks must be taken. Mistakes are part of the risk-taking process. But, the rewards are exciting: Loving relationships, joy, companionship, understanding, and serenity.

Ann D. Clark, <u>Looking Good</u>

Today I will stop brooding—and start meditating.

Nancy T.

Loosening our grip on the past leaves us free to reach for the future.

Ann D. Clark, <u>Alone, But Not Lonely</u>

God is a woman. That's the face I see when I talk to my Higher Power. The aura is feminine to me—it's soft and gentle, and if it had a voice above a whisper, the voice would be soothing, like a breeze.

Jeanne Engelmann, <u>Women and Spirituality</u>

*I will draw on the inexhaustible supply of spiritual energy
that is available to me today and always.*

Anonymous, <u>Inner Harvest</u>

*Still to this day, I never did know why fishing
and menstruating were mutually exclusive.*

Stephanie Ericsson

*When I really look at my hands I am filled with gratitude
and compassion. They work so hard and look so tired.
I rest them, folded, in my lap.*

Martha Cleveland

The child in me says "hold on", the adult in me says "let go".

Harriet Hodgson

My mother sang me through my childhood.

Sefra Kobrin Pitzele

If my toddler is discouraged because he can't yet manipulate
the scissors and cut his paper, I tell him he's trying hard
and that's what counts. When I become discouraged, I scold
and punish myself. The poor little child in me is deprived
of the patience and tolerance I so freely offer to others.
Today I'll take special care of that little girl.
God knows she's waited long enough.

Nancy Hull-Mast

Silence should be used sparingly. But used, nonetheless.

Stephanie Ericsson

Taking care of myself is not selfish—it's essential.

Veronica Ray

Lately, I have more questions than answers. It's painful,
but sometimes breaking out of old beliefs and behaviors is painful.
The only thing that keeps me going is knowing I'm growing.

Liane Cordes

No matter what happens within my family, the most important point is what happens with me. Change myself, not my family.

Amy Dean

I can afford only a short time to examine the hurts in my life.
The faster I move on to forgiveness and understanding,
the faster I will heal and be free to love myself and others.

Suzanne Cusack

*Throughout our lives we make new friends
and care for the ones we've already got.
Old friends know where we've been;
new friends know where we are.
Both help us figure out where we're going.*

Lucinda May

My brain has absolutely no idea that my body is going to pot.
So it still drags my body onto the dance floor; still makes it
climb on a merry-go-round. If you don't tell it, I won't.

Kathleen Rowe

Worry costs me so much and accomplishes nothing.

Pat Samples

Courtesy goes a long way toward expressing love.

Martha Cleveland

Keeping it simple is like taking a canoe downstream. There will be a rush of water, scenery, emotions. There will also be long calm stretches with time to savor the beauty. Keeping it simple is being aware of the current of my life and using it to my advantage.

Patricia Hoolihan

Laughter over our mistakes eases the risk of trying again.
Laughter keeps us young, and the lighthearted find more pleasure
in each day.

Anonymous, <u>Each Day A New Beginning</u>

When my body is an issue for me, it's a sign I'm in emotional or spiritual trouble. When I'm attending to my spirit, I take good care of my body, and I don't think about it much.

Jane Nakken

The Fat Old Mother called Love-yourself-enough
will give you
breath enough
to say what you need to say.

Roseann Lloyd, "Oh," <u>Tap Dancing for Big Mom</u>

My children have a Higher Power and it's not me.

Carolyn White

My fertility can take many forms—each one worthy of my caring and respect.

Jane Rachel Kaplan

We are all responsible for the future of this planet.
I can take personal action to help save it.

Dana L. Wilde

We grow in darkness and in light.

Marilyn J. Mason

*I've learned that my family doesn't pay as much attention to
what I say as to what I do. They watch my feet, not my mouth.*

Stephanie Abbott

Most of us were never told how truly wonderful we are.
We have to find it out for ourselves.

Veronica Ray

Today is enough. I am enough, today.

Carol Slade

I invite food to my meals as a friend, not a lover.

Joan Malerba-Foran

I listen to my inner voices for a course of action in line with who I really am. I don't train for a marathon when I simply want to run five mile races.

Patricia Roth Wuertzer

Empowered women are healthy women connected to other lives by hundreds of sturdy bridges.

Jeanne Engelmann, <u>Women and Spirituality</u>

Control is an illusion. It doesn't work.
Melody Beattie

Letting go of old hurts makes room for new joys.

Sefra Kobrin Pitzele